Kublach Haller

Our campaign face for the 3x World Champion Minnesota Lynx. Brand advocacy helped to increase walk up traffic by 41% during the first season and rocked awareness. Fierce as she looks, All-Star Seimone Augustus was actually yawning in this picture. See more at abdbuzz.com/wnba

Unforgettable influence.

Unforgivably cheap.

$2.4 mil.in earned media from an ad and billboard that never ran.

The cover of <u>The New York Times</u> by throwing a small freak show.

A new liquor category created without a drop of advertising.

Your own influencer channel, created from zip, in 9 months.

Supermodels in a supermarket that stop conversation on *The View*.

This is awareness without advertising.

Figure 1: Campaign thumbnails for The Sharper Image, The City of Excelsior and Barton Brands that collectively generated $3.9.mil. in earned media and 260,000 brand advocates.

TABLE OF CONTENTS

Awareness Without Advertising

Making Buzz That Brands. Bravely.

By Chris C. Birt

Kublach Haller

Who this book is for:

This book is for the owner of a small to middle sized company or a brand manager in a big company. What unites them is anger.

They are both pissed about paying Facebook, Apple, Amazon and others to generate awareness when they know it can be done organically.

They're also impatient. They want something that works faster than "inbound marketing" to fill the top of their sales funnels.

We like to think these people share a "Day One" mentality, or that first day of business when everything matters.

While it won't solve everything, this book will help you solve the one thing that matters most about marketing.

Getting the word out.

With a buzz.

NOTE: There are over 24 charts and graphs in this pocketbook edition They have been downsized to fit. Larger versions can be viewed starting on page 76. Some require viewing online at **abdbuzz.com** where indicated.

"Clean Freaks" for The Sharper Image. From one ad. we achieved above the fold brand advocacy through The New York Times by pairing air cleaners with gritty NY freaks. **See more at** abdbuzz.com/sharperimage

Prologue

Business has discovered bravery as a strategy. Protest ads from Nike, "toxic masculinity" ads from Gillette and #MAGA ads from Donald Trump are all winning™ at what they set out to do. Some call these positions "edgy," I call them buzzy. While someday you'll forget such ads, buzz will remain the best way to build brand awareness without advertising, much.

Growing up in the creative cocoon of Minneapolis, MN did not lead me to this conclusion. I had to work a few detours into Silicon Valley and overseas to broaden my perspective on what makes advertising worth paying for.

Early on, I was great at thinking things up, but not always thinking them through. I soon realized Facebook, Apple, Amazon, Netflix, Google (the FAANGs) were all about the latter. They've figured out everything it takes to make money off you.

As the technologist Shelly Palmer puts it "Google is not a search engine. It is an advertising engine rigged to put the right ad in front of the right person at the right time to optimize revenue for Google. Other considerations are secondary."

I dunno about you, but this makes no sense to me.

This book is focused on how to avoid paying the new "Advertising Man" to generate awareness. This does not mean you can avoid paying for great work. Viral ideas concocted over beers are not sophisticated enough for Silicon Valley.

We are afraid you will have to generate campaign driven content that is likely (but not exclusively) created by advertising professionals. You'll simply use it in a way that optimizes revenue for someone other than Google.

Which is not easily accomplished.

Particularly if you believe the world is rigged.

Sages and Surprises

In this environment, the first goal of a marketer should be to understand, by fiber and strand, how this new online net affects brand awareness. Because now it really doesn't matter what you think, it matters what they think, so you must think things through.

But it doesn't always work that way.

This is because we are the product for the FAANGs. When something is freely provided and then financed by an ingenious advertising scheme you are always their product. They need to have every detail of your life and business posted online to make them money.

Lately, however, people are beginning to unstock themselves from these Silicon Valley shelves. Better yet, more than one of these digital Paladins has looked deeply into their inventory and realized that a lot of it is fake.

Before you concoct a FAANG extortion scheme with your Facebook profile realize that they still police every path you must travel to build awareness. If you want to get anywhere with your brand, therefore, you need to understand the new rules of the road.

While the FAANGs are primarily advertising vehicles they still curate content organically. Their spyders are constantly crawling for "hotspots" of activity and "evergreen" or purely organic activities as well as "high value" conversations and interactions between real people (not robots).

Because of this, we believe the more rigged, inauthentic or just plain fake content grows online, the more FAANGs will reward the opposite kind of content—as they are already doing—to the chagrin of their advertisers.

Without being married to someone named Sergey, Mark, Tim, Jeff or Satya, it is impossible to know precisely what this "opposite" kind of content is.

Conventional wisdom would tell you that it is stuff that is more useful, relevant and actionable. But this is simply the old approach of sucking up to all these guys (where are the women?) precisely when they've suggested you do otherwise.[1]

Our antennae in Silicon Valley point to "other content" that will deliver precisely what their algorithmic machines won't do. They want you *to surprise people*. The Silicon Valley sage George Gilder elaborates on this, citing the latest insights in information theory.

"Information is surprise. If it wasn't surprising, we wouldn't need it. However useful they may be, a machine is not a mind. Human minds can generate counterfactuals, imaginative flights, dreams. By contrast, a surprise in a machine is a breakdown. You don't want surprising outcomes from your machines!"

The FAANGs are aware of their machines' limitations and are aggressively working to neutralize things through Artificial Intelligence (AI).

While they may never become "creative minds," we know FAANG machines are being trained to become more inquisitive. Which makes it theoretically possible to grow awareness with conversations that engage their artificially enhanced curiosity.

If this surprises you, then you really should read this book.

Because things have already moved beyond theory.

---

[1] (Gilder, 2019)

The Online Generation Gap

There is a tendency for those who came of age in web 2.0 to think of digital marketing as axiomatic. Or that "machine learning, artificial intelligence and cloud computing will combine to create a steady cascade of greater capabilities beyond human comprehension."[2]

In other words, marketing is driven by an ever-better sameness until it achieves a perfection we no longer understand. While this fits in perfectly with Silicon Valley schemes, we are reminded of what George Gilder said about machines.

Today a new generation of what might be called web 3.0 (or read/write) thinkers are moving in the opposite direction towards blockchains of information that do not require a FAANG registered imprint to thrive.

Theories aside, it is an inescapable fact that the gap continues to widen between the efficiency of content delivery and the quality of content. Nowhere is this gap more pronounced than with content designed to create awareness, or what we can still conservatively call advertising campaigns.

If you've ever paid Facebook to "boost" a post about your pets (i.e. increase reach and frequency) you'll understand what we mean. Forcing more people into a cringeworthy conversation doesn't always work and yet "petvertising" won't go away.

Part of this is due to 2.0 thought—which has never managed to separate the immense brilliance that goes into creating advertising campaigns—from the act of "advertising" –which is still conventionally understood as paying someone else (i.e. the FAANGs) to get the message out.

---

[2] (Tandoc & Maitra, 2018)

To 2.0 thinkers, advertising is simply content to be made more useful, relevant and engaging to a pre-determined audience that you pay to reach. Some believe ad campaigns have been obsoleted by whitepapers and infographics you send into cyberspace like so many carrier pigeons that eventually return with buckets of leads.[3]

This worked while the internet was a garden of evergreen content. Today everyone is doing it. That's what has Silicon Valley looking for surprises.

Creating Advertising vs. Running It

In the 20th century "advertising" and advertising campaigns were synonymous. While the occasional poster plastered somewhere might generate awareness for free you generally had to pay another business to make your creative output work as "advertising."

The internet changed all this.

Since the internet's inception it has always been possible to create stuff and disseminate it online without paying anyone but an ISP (in the days before coffee shops). As the internet evolved this opportunity declined while remaining less expensive than paying legacy networks and publishers.

Legacy media providers remained expensive till they were obsoleted or acquired from 2005-2012.[4] Yet, ironically, our new media overlords have been acting exactly like the traditional media companies they replaced. They would have you

---

[3] (Loredana, 2017)
[4] (Kaul, 2012)

believe that campaign content will never become "advertising" till you pay them to run it for you. Without their distribution channel, it's all dreck

While they disdain the term "advertising" certain giant marketing automation companies are just as arrogant —they say you can't get your message in front of an audience without their software.[5] At least their model requires real stuff, unlike content farms and fraudsters.

But this is all still basically bullshit.

Content becomes "advertising" when someone else notices it and acts upon it. Today you don't need to pay an intermediary to make that happen.

This means no PPC, no retargeting, no one charging you for the privilege of a faster ride on the information highway.[6] That's because marketing, digital or traditional, is no longer about advertising.

It's about advocacy.

And advocates will work for free.

---

[5] (Loredana, 2017)
[6] (Choi, Jeon, & Kim, 2015)

Projected Advocate Influence

Average 3 shared items per advocate, to 150 friends/colleagues
over a 12 month period

This graphic depicts the potentially exponential reach of advocates. Brand advocacy helps to assure your message expands awareness and leads to conversion on a goal or goals.

A stable of striking original photography and video is critical to brand advocacy. Who wants to share stuff that is underlit and underwhelming?

One. **What Brand Advocacy Is.**

End Goal: **Understand brand advocacy and the hybrid approach.**

Brand advocacy is the process of getting **influential people and organizations** to talk about your brand through **omnichannel media.** It also leverages what is called "**inbound marketing**" to nurture your advocates and your customers.

A search for "brand advocacy" will retrieve a statement like the one below. This definition inaccurately implies that brand advocacy is merely an online phenomenon, but it is still a very workable explanation.

> In electronic commerce and online advertising, a **brand advocate** is a person, or customer who talks favorably about a **brand** or product, and then passes on positive word-of-mouth (WOM) messages about the **brand** to other people. See also the Small Business Marketing Guide in the Quick Reference section of Webopedia.
>
> What is brand advocate? Webopedia Definition
> https://www.webopedia.com/TERM/B/brand_advocate.html

Let's take a closer look at each of brand advocacy's components:

Influential people use media channels to discuss your brand. Unlike straight PR, they usually will reference an advertising campaign that we design for you but do not *pay* an outside organization like Facebook or TV network to distribute.

Inbound marketing is not the first step in brand advocacy but instead the final step that allows you to continually refine your marketing materials and fulfill the needs and wants of your of brand advocates.

As you read our book we will spend a great deal of time discussing the pros and cons of the media mix. Without understanding media, its harder to understand how brand advocacy works.

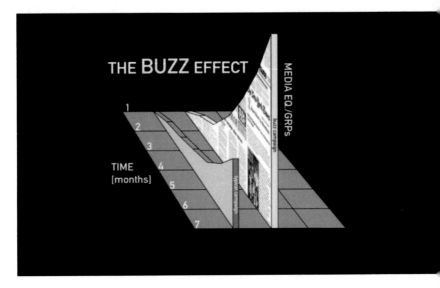

Figure 2: Typical campaign vs. brand advocacy reach and frequency.

Why Brand Advocacy is Free

While nothing is absolutely guaranteed about brand advocacy, it can increase the "reach and frequency" of your message (measured in Gross Rating Points GRPs) very fast and *often for free*.

Brand advocacy generates free awareness because it is driven by shareable content that is *freely distributed*. Creating the content, however, requires hiring professionals to get you started. (Unless you do it yourself).

You will also need to work at keeping your advocacy alive (most important) and your advocates happy (although they change a lot) which once again means paying a few people to help you out.

Let's put this into perspective however. We still live in a world where brand A spends $130 million on advertising while brand B relies on free media, a few ads, and a hairdresser.

We all know how this story ends.

How Jeb Bush Spent $130 Million Running for President With Nothing to Show for It

Jeb Bush at a forum in Columbia, S.C., last week before bowing out of the race for the Republican presidential nomination. Gabriella Demczuk for The New York Times

Figure 3: A world-class example of the need for brand advocacy.

Separating the Advocacy From the Advocate.

We don't believe you should spend all your money on expensive software to help you identify advocates or consultants that can't write or draw either.

At our agency, we've tried pretty much every new piece of software and idea in brand advocacy since 2010. It's all been great to have, but not all that helpful over time. Or maybe we've been too embarrassed to recommend tools like "Ambassify" and "Smarp".

The real reason current approaches to brand advocacy fail is because they don't separate the advocate from the advocacy. While you can point to cave drawings to prove the lasting power of advocacy, we prefer to share the insights of Canadian media professor Marshall McLuhan.

In his seminal work, Understanding Media, he coined two famous terms. "The Global Village" to describe how TV was making the world a smaller place and "the media is the message" to describe how it altered human behavior.

School teachers in McLuhan's time will tell you homework excuses skyrocketed after the price of TVs dropped low enough for everyone to own one.

The funny thing about media, however, is that it can be manipulated to amplify the heck out of a message. Which is why the advocacy itself—or the message – is still more important than the advocate who delivers it. Advocates merely heighten the message by setting it free to take its own course.

McLuhan lived that belief. When his book "The Medium is the Message" (a follow up to Understanding Media) came back from the printer with "Message" spelled as "Massage" he ran with it!

McLuhan's phrase had become so widely accepted by the media pundits, zeitgeist surfers and counterculture heroes of the time, he could play with his creation. Had Professor McLuhan seen himself (advocate) instead of his message (advocacy) as important we would not be talking about him in 2019.

That is why we spend most of our time at the beginning of a campaign analyzing the range of mediums for your message-from the current fads of paid advocates and inbound marketing-to the time-tested hybrid approach of Paid, Earned, Shared and Owned media or PESO.

Figure 4: A comic strip that showcases McLuhan's playful side. While ideas once took years to take hold in the early days of mass media, today they can take seconds to spread. This applies to good ideas as well as bad ones. But what else is new?

Identifying Advocates & Spreading The Word

Figure 5: Chart of archetypes (out of print). [See page 75]

While there are software programs that can help you identify advocates, we find it more useful to identify "personas" that are unique to your market. We spend a great deal of time on this in our focus process (see next chapter).

Additionally, like all agencies that engage in public relations and advertising we maintain our own CRM system for advocates and media that track preferences, sharing profiles, spheres of influence and the like.

Sage Goldnik

GOLDNIQUE

Goldnique is a lifestyle blog
dedicated to the values of
individual style, aspirational
travel and genuine self-
expression. Showcasing Sage's
personal style, grooming and
travel tips, Goldnique has
become the manual for modern
Millennial living.

TOTAL REACH:	AVG BLOG CPE
464K	$0.20

CHAT WITH SAGE

Figure 6: A popular figure on Instagram (circa 2019).

If you have a faddish product or fatuous audience, we will often suggest buying influencer audiences on tapinfluence.com and/or aspirelQ. Tapinfluence can link you to 50,000+ influencers and performance data on people like Sage Goldnik (above) who will lose his influence once he overeats, loses his hair or is exposed by his friends in High School. But seriously, the world has always had paid influencers like Sage who endorse stuff.

In certain fashion circles, these influencers, who work constantly to update their social feeds, blogs, and promotions have supplanted the old guard.

Paid influencers have also emerged in business like Tim Ferrriss ("The Four Hour Work Week"and a record label) Casey Neistadt (Video Blogger) among others. While they are not the new <u>Wall Street Journal</u>, they have impact.

On that note, any conference speaker could become an influencer that promotes you for pay, potentially.

In business, however, you will get more value fom non-paid influencers that maintain a strong media infrastructure to spread the word such as those found in event marketing, wine and spirits, travel destinations, general b to b, and sports.

The most effective brand advocacy is still generated by the editors, analysts and opinion makers paid by media companies to spread the word. They are effective because they are credible.

Figure 7: Tim Ferriss

True buzz travels along corridors of trust that networks of editors, analysts and opinion makers have created over time. These corridors will remain concrete and viable while paid influencers come and go.

Campaign-Driven Media

Buzz, like any living thing, can die off quickly if it is not cultivated. That is why you will need to feed your advocates with "buckets" of campaign-driven tactics and content. While some tactics can be replaced by digital only tactics, a bucket of campaign tactics should include both online and offline media.

In a Jeb-Bush world, massive media buys will always remain a predictable route to awareness. And there's always a $1 million post from Kylie Jenner which is no different than having Joe DiMaggio sell Mr. Coffee (which he did years ago.)

But this is not the real world, which is why new marketing tactics have emerged as worthy competitors to the old. Paid Influencers, particularly those with niche audiences or "nano" influencers, are a viable alternative to paid mass media if their audiences match up with your brand's attributes.

Why Awareness Comes First

It's hard to go into business if you can't get the word out. Generating awareness is at the top of any marketing funnel, yet it's not a top priority for many popular marketing strategies. Here are the three most popular in 2019:

1 **Inbound Marketing** is the process of creating a "customer journey" through precisely targeted articles and blog posts so compelling that customers literally find you. This is a "build it and they will come approach" which works with money, patience and hope.

2 **Product Market Fit** tactics involve creating a minimum viable product that you test and re-test until you can satisfy market needs so insatiable that the product sells itself. It works with enough big data. It's also what Steve Jobs could do in his head.

3 **Influencer Marketing** puts awareness first. We just don't like it when it's forced or inauthentic. Think posts from LinkedIn "Influencers."

While there are myriad marketing tactics available to you today, it just feels like awareness remains delegated to paying the famous or the FAANGs enormous sums to run marginal campaigns that follow you to yoga practice.

And no, you are not imagining that paid media follows you around; it is a very popular technique called ad or content "re-targeting." This involves tracking bots that essentially pick up on your digital footprint once you visit a site and invade your space all over the web till the re-targeting contract runs out.

Or you relent and buy something. Unless it is a car. Then it will never stop.

PESO. The Hybrid Approach.

We're a bit harsh about other marketing tactics because they are marketed as all-or-nothing approaches. Brand Advocacy, on the other hand, is a hybrid that borrows the best ideas from all approaches efficiently and effectively.

Case studies abound on how the use of both "inbound" content and "outbound" brand advocacy can increase return on your marketing investment within a few short months while *reducing* your overall spend.

While marketing savvy businesses and brands today use some form of "hybrid" advocacy they settle for a Prius-caliber media mix when they could be driving a Porsche for a few pennies more. We call this hybrid the PESO paradigm.

PESO stands for "paid, earned, shared, owned," media and segments all marketing channels at a brand's disposal into discrete groups. It allows us to look at our efforts through any one of these four lenses to see if there are opportunities to integrate additional channels into our new or existing programs.

By organizing brand advocacy around this bigger picture, you can more fully exploit opportunities and balance out strengths and weaknesses. The model also allows us to make sense of the channels where we are making our current investments, promote winners and eliminate the losers.

> **Paid Media** is most commonly associated with large media buys and PPC advertising. As we mentioned previously, paid influencers should also be considered a paid channel.

> **Earned Media** is the primary currency of brand advocacy. A highly innovative way to generate earned media is by creating advertising content that journalists and opinion makers report on. A newsworthy advertising campaign is a classic example of this approach.

Shared Media is commonly associated with social media postings on channels like Instagram, Snapchat, Facebook, LinkedIn, Twitter, etc. It is very similar to earned media in most respects.

Owned Media is a true growth area for media. This is the stuff you create yourself with help from professionals. This includes anything you can think of—from a magazine to a full-length movie.

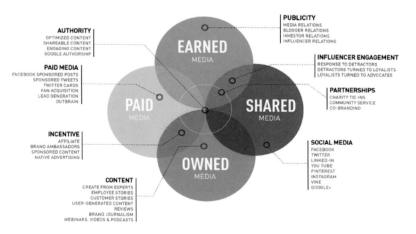

Figure 8 The PESO Model [See page 76]

The above graph shows the breadth and depth of the PESO model. Because it is an "Omnichannel" model, it incorporates both offline and online media and includes opportunities like co-branding, paid partnerships, affiliate marketing, "native advertising" and brand ambassadors.

A strong advertising campaign that can support each of the circles or "buckets" in the model remains the most effective way to generate awareness without paying the new "Advertising Man" for placement.

	Pros	Cons
Paid	• **Scalable**: more money equals more distribution • **Reliable**: guaranteed exposure for your message • **Fast**: media can be placed in front of your audience today	• **Low Trust**: everyone is a bit skeptical of a paid placement or ad • **Expensive**: as reach or frequency increases, so does cost • **Ephemeral**: once you stop investment, returns will drop off quickly
Earned	• **Authoritative**: you are vouched for by a third-party authority • **Cost-Effective Reach**: leverage the size and trust of an established audience • **Long-Term Benefit**: past press mentions or placements can be referenced to create long-term SEO benefits	• **Unreliable**: you can never guarantee a press mention or placement • **Hard to Scale**: does not scale well to global efforts or high volumes of messages • **Expensive**: an effective PR program takes time and/or money to build
Shared	• **High Trust**: people trust their peers more than the media or an ad • **Low Cost**: the amplification of your content is tied to its quality, not the dollars behind it	• **Unreliable**: it is hard to predict what will be shared in advance • **Unscalable**: simply producing more content doesn't always mean more shares
Owned	• **Low Risk**: you can't be shut down when policies change or the platform dies • **Long-Term Asset**: evergreen content will draw audiences as long as it's relevant, your audience will serve you as long as you nurture it	• **Slow**: it takes time to build an audience • **Not Independent**: requires combination with paid, earned, or shared to build an audience

Figure 9: The Pros and Cons of PESO

Campaign-driven brand advocacy offers the pros of paid media with very few cons. In fact, we'll even split hairs with our own PESO chart by calling out that owned media *can* find an audience quickly or that earned media *can* be scaled.

Because brand advocacy continually surprises us. And it will surprise you too.

$2 + MILLION OF ADVOCACY FROM 6K EMAIL AND LETTER CAMPAIGN

This work to launch tourism for the quaint lakeside destination of Excelsior, MN was our first ever brand advocacy campaign. Instead of positioning the spot as bucolic and idyllic we targeted the growing zeitgeist at the time that Starbucks and chains were making everywhere seem like everywhere else.

Resultant earned media extended into the $ millions with coverage on ABC, NBC, CNN, FOX, Newsweek and a documentary on the town that aired on Canadian Public Television. The campaign was voted "Business Story of the Year" by The Business Journals and took the lead in a round up in TIME-magazine which mentioned our practically free campaign in the same breath as a new $25 million campaign for the City of Las Vegas.

What Brand Advocacy is Not

Brand advocacy is different than "word-of-mouth" because it requires you to build a stable of content that is brand driven. This may include, but is not limited to, a branded ID, 30 second video spots, short films, a soundtrack, banner ads, text only ads, whitepapers and an avalanche of pictures, memes and posts.

Brand advocacy is also focused on leveraging "words" that already exist—or what we call leveraging other people's audiences (LOPA).

Signs of A Brand Advocacy Impostor:

1. They tell you it is purely word-of-mouth
2. They tell you it is all digitally driven—or the glorified intersection of influencers and advocates that you cultivate and pay to say nice things about you online.
3. They sell you on advocates instead of advocacy.
4. They sell you on advertising like PPC (and that is just for starters).
5. Their whole spiel just feels inauthentic.

Brand advocacy differs from purely digitally driven advocacy in its assumption that content creates its own awareness. It is closest in practice to the way a novelist develops a "readership."

We've already pointed out the promise and pitfalls of paid advocates a.k.a. "influencers." We will always look upon them skeptically along with many of our peers in the advertising, public relations and publicity profession.

Pundits are already questioning the staying power of these self-made celebrities. While they have followers galore everyone knows the deal is quid pro quo. If everyone is doing it, soon no one will be getting anywhere.

Our biggest issue with paid advocates is their lack of spontaneity and surprise. Advocates feel fulfilled by finding stuff and delivering it to their audience. That is why paid influencers come and go, but true, trusted advocates with a following will remain relevant and valuable to brands.

Figure 10: Why people share stuff online.

MOVEMBER

Lorenzo Lucid
Follow · November 17, 2012

Like · Share

 4 people like this.

Sheila McGregor ...wow...so nice it almost looks fake...
November 17, 2012 at 3:30pm · Like

Ginny Marie Herman Ohh Lorenzo, you are so handsome. Wait. There is something different about you.
November 18, 2012 at 10:13am · Like

Lorenzo Lucid I've been lifting
November 19, 2012 at 2:33pm · Like

Lorenzo Lucid, the original "faux advocate" for Lucid Brewing who soared to 5700 likes, 3 marriage proposals and 17 requests for more personal information about status before we blew his cover on BuzzFeed. See more at abdbuzz.com/lorenzo

Two: Focus|Clarity|Dimension

End Goal: See the big picture for brand advocacy.

The Process Your Peers Are Using.

By now you should have a clear understanding of what brand advocacy is. The rest of this book will cover how to create it through the process of focus, clarity and dimension.

This process has one aim—to help you generate immediate and sustained awareness. We depict this process with a painting that we commissioned at our founding. Hundreds of companies have seen themselves at some point in this picture. Go to **abdbuzz.com/baware** to see for yourself.

Figure 11: Our painting that depicts a process. [see more on page 77]

Focus is a matrix driven method which separates your corporate perceptions from customer realities. You will input your own information and information from outside sources to determine your Minimum Viable Truths (MVTs) to put to the test. It requires you to make bold decisions based on limited information about advocates and advocacy.

Focus should be completed in a business quarter.

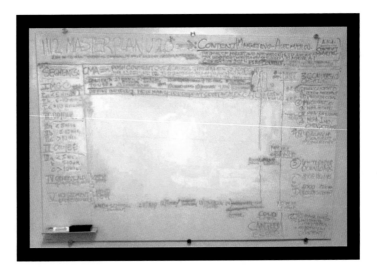

Figure 12: Rough whiteboard generated during focus.

Clarity is the refining step in our process. It is funnel-based and linear. It requires you to clarify your minimum viable truth (or truths) down to one essential truth, which is hard to do.

The clarity phase usually involves a limited run of online testing that can last from 7-21 days. In this phase you will test your MVTs 3 at a time to 3 advocate or real personas through email messaging, live ad concepts and landing pages that you score for results.

Clarity is an exercise in sacrifice that is going to burn a little before it comes together. Steven Spielberg has said "If you can't write out your movie idea on a matchbook, you don't have an idea."

Clarity is on-going. You will know it when you see it.

Dimension involves articulating and disseminating your essential truth through omnichannel techniques. While it puts the premium on owned and earned techniques it may eventually involve paid media based upon your ambitions.

The dimension phase also involves ongoing monitoring and measurement of your campaigns. Remember that this is a process and not a project. We will usually create up to 3 dashboards for you to analyze the performance of your core content, your social media performance and a master dashboard that incorporates offline and/or traditional metrics.

You should be able to achieve a projectable level of awareness without paying for media. Reading this book will help you achieve this goal.

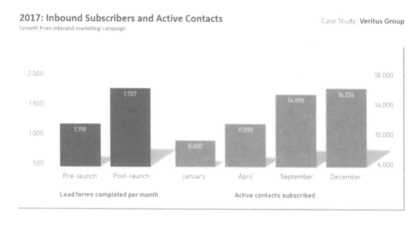

2017: Inbound Subscribers and Active Contacts
Growth from inbound marketing campaign

Case Study **Veritus Group**

Figure 13: Inbound leads without outbound advertising.

Wide Eye for Barton Brands. This campaign for a caffeinated schnapps was launched without TV. All video and radio spots were webcast in local bar chains. Variations were rigorously tested during the Clarity phase of our process. See more at abdbuzz.com/wideeye

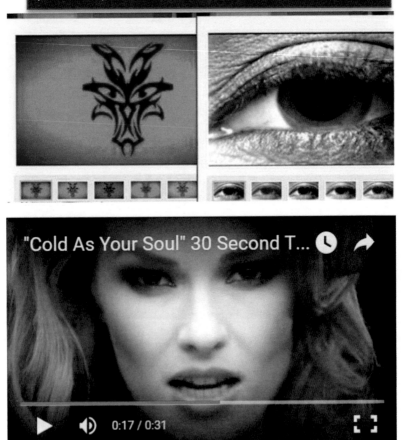

"Cold As Your Soul" 30 Second T... 🕐 ➤

▶ 🔊 0:17 / 0:31

Three: Focus

End Goal: Discern between PMF and MZF.

Welcome to focus. Some people find this the most exhilarating part of our process, while others find it a bit esoteric. Fortunately, the focus matrix does lend itself to a clear demarcation between the art and science of brand advocacy and it is efficient at generating Minimum Viable Truths (MVTs).

The Focus Matrix

The planning phase of focus is depicted in the matrix below. Here you will think about your goals in terms of quadrants, a series of interlocking circles and the interrelationships between each.

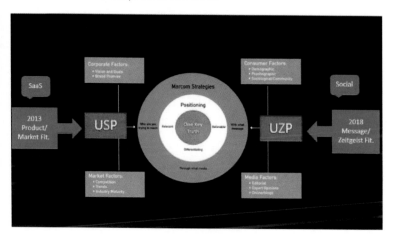

Figure 14: The focus matrix. [See page 78]

Quadrants and Circles

The Focus matrix captures information in four quadrants: corporate, market, demographic and media. It is important to fill each quadrant with accurate information. *The matrix should be populated in about a week.*

The circular portions of the matrix are designed to help you think up brand truths that are relevant, believable and differentiating. It is risky to rely purely on your own assumptions. Focus generates testable truths that help you objectively assess message strengths, weaknesses and opportunities.

> "It's really hard to design products by focus groups. A lot of times, people don't know what they want until you show it to them."
>
> — Steve Jobs

If you are really pressed for time, then you can jump directly to the essential questions that must be asked of any marketing effort:

Who are we trying to reach? Using the quadrants, you will fill in people you believe are important for advocacy, with help from a professional.

Through which media? You will use the PESO paradigm to balance the media mix, with help from a media planner that understands the metaverse.

With what message? While it is possible for you to generate this critical piece on your own, it pays to have a professional with the winnowing.

None of these questions will be helpful if you cannot get the ultimate question out of the way.

What are you trying to accomplish?

If you don't know the answer to this question you might want to go away and do a rethink. You will know your answer once you can clearly articulate your objective and how the art and science of brand advocacy might help you achieve it.

That means translating something like this:

"I want to sell a million shoes, fast."

Into something like this:

"I want to create a market for edible footwear now that Crocs has abandoned their niche. I will invest in 1, 3 and 6 month-tests to build awareness fast."

This will also outline business problems that brand advocacy can't solve.

We were once hired by a non-profit client that thought they needed awareness when their real problem was a lack of mentors. Once they realized their goal was to find mentors who would work hard for free, we told them to invest more of our fees with their talent recruiting firm.

The Art and Science of Creating MVTs

The real locus of focus is the Product Market Fit (PMF) and the Message Zeitgeist Fit (MZF). These are "best-of-breed" approaches for your MVTs, your Essential Truth and successful brand advocacy.[7]

The PMF path is, ostensibly, the more scientific way to arrive at your MVTs. The UZP path is more instinctual. It is important to understand both.

Product Market Fit (circa 2013)

Companies once focused marketing departments on isolating unique selling propositions (USP) that today can be called the Product Market Fit (PMF).

 A classic example is the early TV advertising for aspirin when Ted Bates Agency successfully positioned Excedrin for headache relief. The USP was unique but it was barely supported by data.

Most innovative companies today rely less on human insight and more on arbitraging big data to arrive at the ideal Product Market Fit to create a position.

A classic PMF is how Airbnb successfully integrated its service with Craigslist in 2004. This case study has become a somewhat legendary example of what they call "growth hacking" in Silicon Valley that involved finding a way into the Craig's List API—or backdoor to their data. Without data generated by the classified pages of the internet (Craigslist) there may not have been an Airbnb.

---

[7] (Awad & Fatah, 2015) (Berghofer, Hofbauer, & Sangl, 2018) (Wilder, 2015) (Gilder, 2019)

Airbnb staff constantly monitored new usage data from Craigslist to isolate key MVTs. These included *"rental apartments are messy"* and *"renting from an owner is cheaper than renting from a company"*.

These are not so much truths as they are data-driven statements of fact. Airbnb staff, in turn, used this data to drive advocacy by leveraging it for blogging, editorial and social media opportunities.

It is possible to build a brand advocacy campaign around the PMF model. On the surface this may appear the most predictive of the two approaches.

On a deeper level, however, it requires a precise alignment of other forces to make it work. In this sense, it is the unicorn of the two approaches.

That's because Product Market Fit advocates aren't really into hatching new ideas as much as they are *hitching rides on products that already exist.* It can be shameless the way this happens, but if your stars are aligned it can work.

Today advanced metrics programs offer myriad ways to analyze online behavior. PMF advocates hope this data will yield that killer insight or "aha moment" that leads to a product that effectively sells itself.

The Sharing is the Message. Sometimes.

Interestingly, while online products can't always "sell themselves," they can be designed to promote themselves. The difference between spreading a headache and a hit is to design "good stuff" that is engineered to be shared.

PMF advocate Ivan Kirigin says, "if your product involves sharing at its core, you should focus on *encouraging* it." DropBox grew by giving away free storage to users who shared their service. HotMail achieved growth along similar lines.

Archie Abrams at high growth firm Udemy continues this train of thought. "Companies that win find a channel like email, Facebook notifications or push notifications that can sustainably drive users back to their product." Of course, if you think this sounds like online marketing you are not alone.

Archie Abrams
VP of Product at Udemy

My name is Archie, and I'm the VP of Product at Udemy!

I joined Udemy in January 2012 as the 10th employee (we're now 280!). Before moving to Product, I used to lead our Growth team which was responsible for student acquisition and retention. I built the Growth team from 1 (me!) to 25.

Before Udemy I was founder and CEO of Amplify Teaching, an Edtech company based in Boston, and a strategy consultant.

in

Figure 15: Creating Brand Advocacy through USP|PMF means you'll cross paths with people like Archie. And you won't need this book, because your product will sell itself.

Message Zeitgeist Fit (2018)

The best way to generate awareness without advertising relies more on big ideas than big data. A brand's market fit is often less important than its relationship to a zeitgeist for brand advocacy.

"What is the future? I will answer that the future is here. It's just not widely distributed yet."

--William Gibson

Zeitgeists are the "spirits of a time"[8] that can be latently or explicitly observed in a culture; particularly in communities online.[9] Random events are influenced by larger dynamics. Cultural clues yield incredible insights for messaging. Social archetypes reveal patterns of conversations.

Our stable of case studies at ABdigital is based around this proposition. Time and again we have generated awareness by relating a brand message to zeitgeists "not widely distributed" yet.[10]

While not our campaign, the use of Colin Kaepernick as the face of Nike for the 2018 NFL Season is instructive. By leveraging Kapernick's image in a large close up shot and the politics of social protest, Nike created a 31% increase in online sales in the following business quarter.

---

[8] (Ventura, 2018)

[9] (Boyd, 2008)

[10] See www.abdbuzz.com: American Express, Constellation Brands, The Sharper Image, WNBA et. al

Gillete recently created a media flurry by creating an ad campaign that re-examined the position of "The Best a Man Can Get" by questioning the meaning of masculinity. Like Nike, they received a backlash along political lines, but their sales increased for a time.

A textbook example of zeitgeist positioning is Donald Trump's use of #MAGA which tapped into the zeitgeist of the "Silent Majority. While his detractors may still prove the KGB elected him, we're putting our money on his MZF.

Always Push for "Surprising Solutions."

The jazz pioneer (and former poolroom shark, vaudevillian and hustler) Jelly Roll Morton wrote his seminal, "Black Bottom Stomp" in 1926. The song solved the problem of how to create interest and drama in just under three minutes.

His solutions? *Think architecturally: carefully plot themes and sections, differentiate an introduction. Juxtapose 11 different textural combinations and vary the rhythm of each. Hire the best musicians, and much more.*[1]

We often look at musicians as classic readers of the Zeitgeist. Jelly Roll Morton, for example, ushered in modern jazz long before the advent of marketing professionals.

Celebrities ride for SWT. The local bus company had a problem: it just was not cool to ride the bus. This campaign featured local and national celebrities that made it safe for social climbers to hop on board. See more at abdbuzz.com/celebsride.

FUNNY PEOPLE RIDE
SO CAN YOU.

Four: **Clarity**

The Clarity Funnel & Brand Advocates

Once you have staged your goals and arrived at your Minimum Viable Truths, you are ready for clarity, or more specifically, for the Clarity Funnel. The Clarity Funnel helps you test your MVTs till you arrive at your one essential truth.

The most efficient way to commence this "winnowing" process is to create advocate personas which can be real people (that represent a demographic or position) or composite sketches. Advocate personas help you think clearly about your message, how it connects to a zeitgeist, and to the people who mold and shape it.

Whether real or representative, advocate personas are generated from demographic *and* psychographic information. Some digerati and designers are fond of decking out personas with cool names and clothing choices.

Or you can just point to Betty Crocker.

We find this kind of effort useful to the extent that it gets you thinking about messaging potentials and constraints.[11]

---

[11] Different industries respond to different tactics. See recent data measured across 423 discrete industries (source: SEMrush: 2018)

Advocate Personas & The Funnel

The Clarity Funnel is designed to capture minimally predictive information about your messaging. It also serves as a key step in "mapping" an advocate journey that is constantly refreshed and refined (see next chapter).

We've seen companies spend even more time on creating journey "maps" than they do on personas. While the journey is important, it is more important to test ideas to "plan" the trip. This is where we rely on real micro campaigns, replete with content, that you test against advocate personas.

Figure 16: Example of a simple clarity funnel with 3 advocate personas and 3 MVTs to test with landing pages. This chart depicts the use representative personas, not real people [See page 79]

Are You There Yet?

Clarity is the part of our process when the gates open and the route to awareness without advertising appears. At least that is what is supposed to happen.

All of this is possible provided you can master one essential thing—to get your Minimum Viable Truths down to one. This is an exercise in sacrifice, compounded by the fact you will be choosing from a range of equally valid truths. The good news is that you don't have to do this on your own.

Working Through 3s

Clarity begins with choices. At our agency we often say that there are no wrong choices in marketing, just some that are "more right" than others. That is why it is critical in focus to have a professional bring your Minimum Viable Truths to life through words, pictures and video.

It ultimately comes down to showing and testing real concepts against a real audience to truly understand what you have.

The "micro campaigns" we mentioned a few paragraphs earlier are not just a few words on a screen. They are at least **3 concepts** taken to finished stage to help you think through the implications and impact of your MVTs. We then set up an online "Funnel Test" to gauge reaction against an advocate base for at least **3 weeks**.

Map Content to the Buyer's Journey

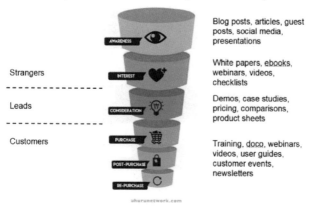

Figure 17: A "Buyer's Journey" funnel. Seen one, you've seen them all.

While the timing of this phase will vary, you can gain some predictive information in 7 – 21 days. This information, in turn, is used to clarify your one essential truth, your advertising campaign (that you don't run) and direction for your content.

The Advocate Journey. Redux.

Generating awareness without advertising requires bold action in the face of uncertainty. This is where we may circle back to the advocate's "journey" (like a "Buyer's Journey, see above). When we test MVTs, we not just looking for high open rates on emails or video views but how well they support the key touchpoints of a journey.

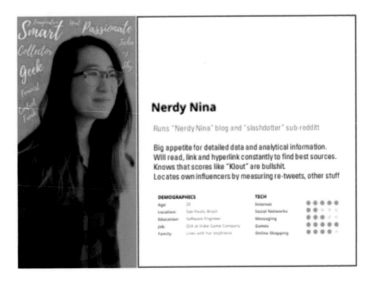

Figure 18: Advocate persona targeted by interests

Those touchpoints can be measured more quantitatively than qualitatively. Unlike a few years ago, today you can score quantitative information from a landing page and 2-3 test concepts as quickly as you can compile a Facebook page. While we don't create a "fixed map" of those touchpoints, a tour guide of sorts can be exceptionally useful.

While the details will change from advocate to advocate, brand to brand and zeitgeist to zeitgeist, mapping out the advocate journey with quantitative findings will harden your essential truth. More general compass than GPS, it is still brand advocacy implemented at the most granular level.

"Lil' Miquela," the first totally artificial influencer to reach a million followers on Instagram (2019). See more at abdbuzz.com.

5: Dimension

End Goal: A sense for media and analytics.

Dimension is the final phase of our process and a donkey kick to the legs of your essential truth. A weak truth leads to pain. A strong truth leads to performance.

That is why we encourage our clients to think about the metaverse for marketing. The metaverse describes the online conversations that are indirectly related to your product, brand or service. Your goal is to inject a new voice into those conversations and steer them more your way.

If your brand is attracting a high level of influencer interest, being actively shared by high-value people, and showing lengthy session time, the FAANGs will elevate your brand message organically. Content that creates its own advocates, after all, equals more advertising revenue for the FAANGs.

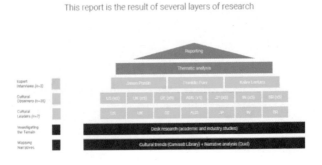

Figure 19: A report on "Good Censorship" from Google [See page 80]

The previous chart illustrates a recent project by Google that outlines how they go about "mapping narratives". Keep in mind that this is an active process to determine what is elevated on their site and what is pushed down. This project, called "The Good Censor," is pertinent to media planning today.

Assuming your message is built well (based upon a single essential truth) then the goal of a media planner today is to map out the potential intersection of brand advocacy and online narratives to generate earned media.

The Media Mix

Brand advocates are your best channel for generating earned media. Your goal as a marketer is to give them something they can share. The chart below depicts a campaign we created for a chain of bars and restaurants. While we designed out-of-home and advertising materials we never paid to place them and used their own bar channel and social channels for brand advocates.

Figure 20: Content bucket in a big budget campaign.

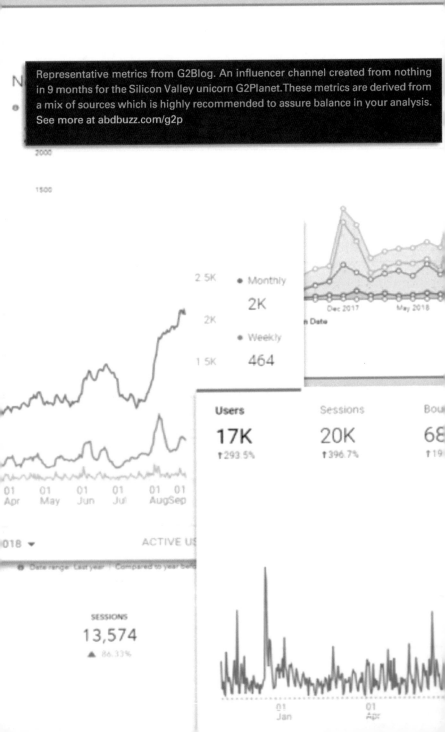

N

2000

1500

2.5K • Monthly
      2K
2K
      • Weekly
1.5K   464

Dec 2017   May 2018

n Date

01   01   01   01   01 01
Apr May Jun Jul AugSep

018 ▼   ACTIVE US

Date range: Last year Compared to year befo

Users   Sessions   Bou
17K   20K   68
↑293.5%   ↑396.7%   ↑19

SESSIONS
13,574
▲ 86.33%

01   01
Jan   Apr

PESO and the "Data-Driven" Approach.

Brands today have a "data-driven" obsession. PESO has become a very popular model in marketing precisely because it measures so many variables:

Paid Media: Exchanging money for distribution, whether an ad or content.

Earned Media: Trading valuable content for an authority's audience.

Shared Media: Amplifying content through your own audience.

Owned Media: Aggregating an audience for content.

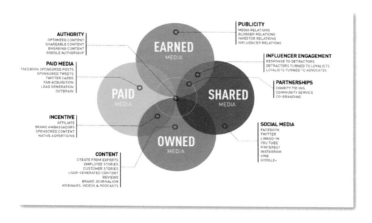

Figure 21: The PESO model.

PESO requires constant monitoring and measurement although the amount of data it requires to generate insights may not require a mainframe to contain.

PESO Analytics

How much awareness do you need to accomplish your business goals? The answer to this question is different for every brand, product or service.

Whatever your awareness goals may be, the modern way to monitor campaign effectiveness is to measure **conversion goals** This generally means anything you can tie to a specific action like a download, editor inquiry or sales call.

To keep things organized, we group analytics into three areas of focus.

Area One: **Omnichannel Analytics.**

Analytics *are* multilayered and complex. That is why we encourage clients to follow just a few key metrics on their website and set up simple conversion goals to get started. Visit Google Analytics for tutorials that cover the basics.

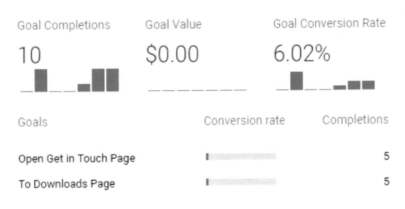

Figure 22: Simple conversion goals on the Google dashboard.

From this foundation we will then create customized dashboards. While details will vary, measuring the PESO mix requires at least three dashboards:

The first dashboard should measure your blog performance on a granular level. Metrics will proceed from the general to the specific

Figure 23: Dashboard that tracks general engagement. [See page 81 & 82]

Google Analytics: Top Landing Pages

Account: Major Gift Academy | View: All Web Site Data | Traffic channel: All | Segment: All Users | Period: 14 Jan - 20 Jan, 2019

No.	Landing Page	Sessions ▼	% New Sessions	New Users	Bounce Rate	Pages / Session	Avg. Session Duration
1	/academy/	199 (30.03%)	69.15%	130 (47.45%)	78.19%	1.45	00:00:59
2	/login/	116 (19.53%)	16.38%	19 (6.93%)	17.24%	5.36	00:07:11
3	/	80 (12.78%)	58.75%	47 (17.15%)	40.00%	3.27	00:02:39
4	/courses-home/	49 (7.63%)	10.20%	5 (1.82%)	28.57%	4.31	00:05:03
5	/ACADEMY/	46 (7.35%)	45.65%	21 (7.66%)	69.57%	1.57	00:02:21

Once you drill down deeper on Dashboard One you will generate information on landing pages that create the most session time, posts that lead to conversions, dwell time on post, video shares, follow-on posts and even the performance of ads vs. organic content.

This type of dashboard does not provide a true omnichannel view of awareness. It is, however, incredibly useful at helping you measure what content is working most effectively on your site.

When you combine this dashboard with a marketing automation system like Hubspot you can get a closer look at how this site activity converts to leads

The second dashboard should append your blog and site performance to your performance across social and interactive channels.

Figure 24: Social metrics dashboard.

This type of dashboard focuses heavily on what is called "off page SEO" and isolates channels that generate the highest quality traffic and engagement. Among other metrics, it helps to determine:

- Which social networks create visitors that spend time on your site.
- Which networks generate return visitors.
- Which mobile devices generate quality visits.
- Bounce Rate by Social Network.
- Goal Conversions by Social Network.
- **And numerous other social metrics and mobile device stats.**

By now you could be thinking "that's a lot of dashboards, just give me one." While it's true that an omnichannel media mix should have a single dashboard to keep things simple, it is not always feasible.

You also might notice that we use a variety of systems to create dashboards and that the UI (User Interface) changes. This is because there is no "one size fits all" vendor for analytics. Which leads us back to the original lodestar.

Your third dashboard should be created entirely in Google Analytics, tweaked to measure online and offline channels. No more, no less.

We've chased every new development in analytics the past decade, from KISS Metrics (behavioral metrics), Meltwater (expensive PR metrics) SEMRush, Hootsuite, Facebook and Instagram tools and more.

They all measure, in one way or another, what you can measure in Google Analytics if given enough time. Whatever Google overlooks, they eventually incorporate into their platform (i.e. cohort behavior, look alikes).

Today's analytics platforms can inexpensively pull data from about ten sources into one dashboard at a time. Which is plenty. Our advice, then, is to rock Google Analytics and support it with a dashboard or two that allows you to drill down on the PESO metrics that matter most.

Area Two: Integrated Offline Analytics

Simmons Research is the gold standard for measuring traditional media. We have used Simmons to measure up to 40 different digital media activities alongside traditional TV, magazines, radio and outdoor.

Cision and Meltwater are the predominant platforms for measuring classic public relations. Sadly, the FAANGs are rendering the media they measure obsolete. Google Analytics and a supplementary dashboard can be taught to follow all the same stuff—especially earned media, conversation density and "talk signals" or what influencers *might* say.

Area Three: Self-Learning Systems & Automation

Workflows are used to generate data about prospects while automating the process of sending emails and white papers. Lead scoring is a more advanced form of workflow that provides granular data about prospects. We believe Hubspot and Ontraport have the best tutorials on how to set these systems up.

In our next volume of <u>Awareness Without Advertising</u>, we take a much deeper dive into analytics and how to use them for brand advocacy. This book has been written to get you to the point where you have something to analyze.

For example, we once worked for a huge HMO that had an entire staff devoted to analyzing prototype sites that generated about 300 sessions. It is impossible to gain predictive information from a data set that small.

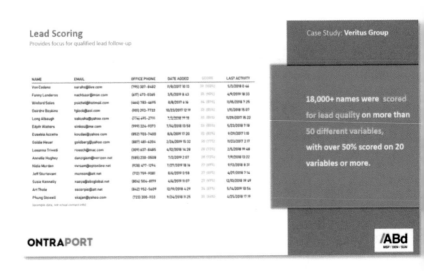

Figure 25:Useful processes like lead scoring are an ongoing essential. This is an example of how a content bucket can continually yield insights.

While the range varies by client, we would say that 750 sessions (unique visitors to a site) is robust enough to be predictive. Anything less than that requires only the basic stuff that comes with a Wordpress or similar site.

If you are not generating activity above this level, you have other issues at stake. While re-organizing your marketing department or firing your agency might assuage the pain, hiring a new brand advocacy hotshot can still leave you in hot water from a sales perspective.

You will need a Customer Relationship Management (CRM) system to help you close the loop and bring things full circle.

You Are What You Eat for Lunds & Byerly's, a chain of high-end grocery stores in the Midwest. This concept pioneered the idea of food as fashion and was launched with a full runway show in a new supermarket, replete with Supermodels. See more at abdbuzz/byerlys

6: From Awareness to Action

End Goal: Using MQLs SQLs and getting your data into a CRM.

Generating awareness will fill the top of your sales funnel with potential leads. You will then use some common analytics processes to qualify and eventually score those leads derived from a PESO mix of media. If these steps are done properly, the only thing left is to close deals. Although that rarely happens.

Setting up workflows and lead scoring systems takes time. Typical conversion goals measure online downloads and blog subscriptions. While it is probable that someone who downloads a whitepaper and subscribes to your blog is a quality prospect, the opposite is possible.

While you can continue to qualify leads online or through your workflows, you will eventually want to reach out to your prospects directly. It is critical that your conversion data integrates with your CRM to make this happen.

MQLs and SQLs

Hubspot has coined a variety of terms that are universally applicable to lead management and conversion. We like the terms Market Qualified Leads (MQLs) and Sales Qualified Leads (SQLs).

An MQL is a lead that has met enough goals in a workflow (or a sequence of actionable items) to be handed off to sales. At the most granular level the art and science of advocacy is about amassing maximum MQLs for a minimal investment. Converting your MQLs into SQLs simply requires you to convert all that data into a CSV file you input into Salesforce. To close deals it is therefore critical that you work with your marketing team to properly align your marketing information with the key metrics in your CRM.

All the major marketing automation platforms today integrate easily with Salesforce although not all of them provide real time data sharing.

Generally, the level of integration of your "MQLs" into your CRM system will be dictated by the size and scope of your salesforce automation efforts. Clearly the real-time integration of MQLs with your CRM is the best way to nurture leads and close deals but it is not essential

Nurturing Awareness

The ultimate benefit of following an awareness campaign from the first signs of interest to the final sale is educational. You learn a great deal about your brand message and how it should evolve.

Ultimately, however, it is impossible to deduce from a lead score how valuable a prospect is. That can only be known, once a customer clicks the buy button, requests a sales call or a demo.

In our next book we will go into greater detail about how you can use lead scoring to convert more customers. If you are wondering why we did not just start there, we have a simple reason.

Without awareness there are no leads.

That's why we started, and will finish, with this book.

MARBLED

LIKE A TRUMP
BATHROOM

100ᵗʰ NATIONAL WESTERN Stock Show

Brand advocacy for the National Western. The "animals as rock stars" campaign generated the largest attendance in history for this legendary event with over 744,000 attendees. See more at abduzz.com/NWSS

Epilogue

We have a saying at our agency that "it is better to be decisive than certain" when you think about business and the future.

Despite AI, Big Data and Big Mark et. al. no marketing approach will ever be 100% predictive or decisive until the robots really do take over. If that happens none of us will be around to worry about it anyway.

The more you practice the principles in this book the closer you will inch from creating a few advocates to establishing a community of followers.

Because brand advocacy done right goes big. Bigger in proportion to your investment than any other strategy for brand awareness today.

Of that, we are certain.

Decisively.

Brand advocacy for the apartments once inhabited by Bob Dylan. Sometimes the zeitgeist just stares you in the face. Inexplicably, the developers had played up bus service in their previous campaign.

Please enjoy a few "fave" advocacy snapshots on the following pages.

ent from anywhere else. When Bob Dyla
t of a landmark apartment called FloCo
nd other sweet juxtapositions make us

Advocacy Snapshot: Lunds & Byerly's

One of our very first campaigns for this upscale grocer introduced the concept of food/fashion. The idea was innovative enough to be copied by the Target Corporation that ran a distinctly similar theme in Houston, TX.

We launched our campaign with a 45-minute fashion show in a supermarket with models wearing custom clothes adorned with food. (Note: shrimp cocktail headdress and the "sush-ski" depicted.)

Passionate advocates coalesced around the campaign that targeted a zeitgeist of food as a fashion statement. The idea was feted' by Joy Behar on The View and received major local and national coverage.

Brand advocacy for Byerly's has since been featured in The American Review of Advertising and, ironically, handbooks used by Target.

Advocate Snapshot: Barton Brands

"Demented" is how NPRs Lynne Rosetto Kasper described our campaign for Wide-Eye Caffeinated Schnapps from the parent of Corona Beer. This product was successfully launched last fall in 14 markets across the country and quickly shot to the #3 bar mixed shot in five DMAs.

Ms. Kasper (whom we know and love) was referring to the product itself, but her comments lead to more buzz that culminated in lines stretching outside the International Wine & Spirits Show in Las Vegas just to taste it. A first.

Advocacy Snapshot: Lucid Brewing

Lucid Brewing has become a keynote case study for advocacy. Not only was our original (and very fake) advocate's cover blown by his creator a few weeks after we created both the brand, the blog and the site from SCRATCH, but the Brewery blew past all sales records for a regional brewery making it to *2000 barrels in its first year.*

This campaign targeted the opposite of the current "craft beer" zeitgeist and borrowed cues from Italian and modernist design.

Advocacy Snapshot: The MPL

"The Minneapolis Public Library – has a new ad campaign out to hype the new downtown library. One side of the poster has a big picture of Mao; beneath him, it says, well, MAO. On the other side, a picture of the new library, with the letters MPL, for Minneapolis Public Library. What's the connection? Mao was a former librarian. Albeit one who favored only one book, unlike the MPL.

The campaign also features J. Edgar Hoover and Batgirl, because they, like Mao, were librarians at some point in their lives. It's a stretch and a little weird, but it made us look and that's the point."

© Skyway News, 2013

This simple post in a local business site elicited comments from tsunami of national and international bloggers, including "hidebound anti-Communists" and the MPL opened to huge success. **The campaign simply targeted the reverse of the "boring librarian" archetype**.

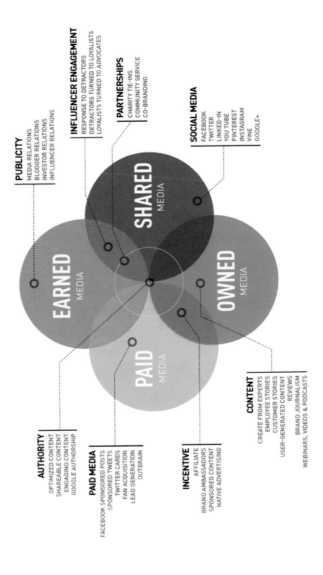

PUBLICITY
MEDIA RELATIONS
BLOGGER RELATIONS
INVESTOR RELATIONS
INFLUENCER RELATIONS

INFLUENCER ENGAGEMENT
RESPONSE TO DETRACTORS
DETRACTORS TURNED TO LOYALISTS
LOYALISTS TURNED TO ADVOCATES

PARTNERSHIPS
CHARITY TIE-INS
COMMUNITY SERVICE
CO-BRANDING

SOCIAL MEDIA
FACEBOOK
TWITTER
LINKED-IN
YOU TUBE
PINTEREST
INSTAGRAM
VINE
GOOGLE+

AUTHORITY
OPTIMIZED CONTENT
SHAREABLE CONTENT
ENGAGING CONTENT
GOOGLE AUTHORSHIP

PAID MEDIA
FACEBOOK SPONSORED POSTS
SPONSORED TWEETS
TWITTER CARDS
FAN ACQUISITION
LEAD GENERATION
OUTBRAIN

INCENTIVE
AFFILIATE
BRAND AMBASSADORS
SPONSORED CONTENT
NATIVE ADVERTISING

CONTENT
CREATE FROM EXPERTS
EMPLOYEE STORIES
CUSTOMER STORIES
USER-GENERATED CONTENT
REVIEWS
BRAND JOURNALISM
WEBINARS, VIDEOS & PODCASTS

SHARED MEDIA
EARNED MEDIA
OWNED MEDIA
PAID MEDIA

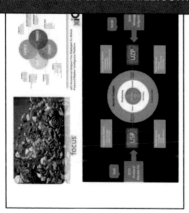

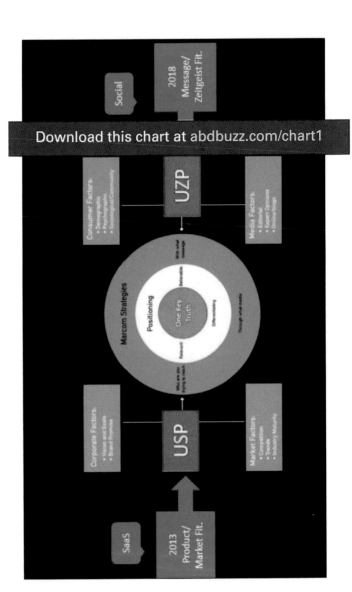

Download this chart at abdbuzz.com/chart1

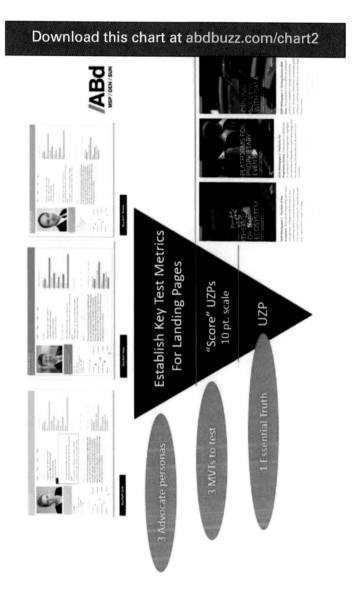

Establish Key Test Metrics For Landing Pages

"Score" UZPs
10 pt. scale

UZP

3 Advocate personas

3 MVTs to test

1 Essential Truth

This report is the result of several layers of research

Traffic Analytics: Summary

Visits	**Unique Visitors**	**Pages / Visit**
13.8K +96.29%	**11.7K** +67.39%	**1.56** +56.34%
Avg. Visit Duration	**Bounce Rate**	**Traffic Rank**
02:58 n/a	**67.30%** -32.70%	**1611108** ↑1142131

Traffic Analytics: Traffic Sources Trend

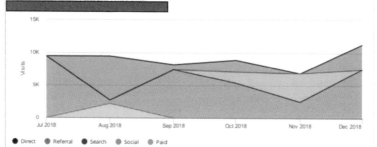

● Direct ● Referral ● Search ● Social ● Paid

Traffic Analytics: Metrics Chart (Visits)

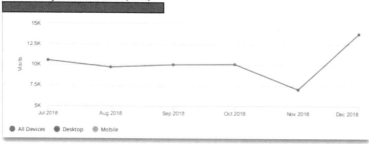

● All Devices ● Desktop ● Mobile

Google Analytics: Top Landing Pages

| View: All Web Site Data | Traffic channel: All | Segment: All Users | Period: 14 Jan - 20 Jan, 2019

No.	Landing Page	Sessions ▼	% New Sessions	New Users	Bounce Rate	Pages / Session	Avg. Session Duration
1	/academy/	188 (30.03%)	69.15%	130 (47.45%)	78.19%	1.45	00:00:59
2	/login/	116 (18.53%)	16.38%	19 (6.93%)	17.24%	5.36	00:07:11
3	/	80 (12.78%)	58.75%	47 (17.15%)	40.00%	3.27	00:02:39
4	/courses-home/	49 (7.83%)	10.20%	5 (1.82%)	28.57%	4.31	00:05:03
5	/ACADEMY/	46 (7.35%)	45.65%	21 (7.66%)	69.57%	1.57	00:02:21

82

Bibliography:

Awad, T. A., & Fatah, S. M. (2015). The Impact of Social Media Branding on Developing Brand Advocates for Start-Ups. *Journal of Online Marketing, 5*, 37-59.

Banfield, Jerry; Gerard, Michel. (2016). *Facebook Marketing and Advertising in 2016: What works for my page with 2 million likes?*

Berghofer, F., Hofbauer, G., & Sangl, A. (2018). Indicators to Choose a Suitable Marketing Automation Platform. *International Journal of Management Science and Business Administration, 4*, 52-60.

Boyd, J. K. (2008). *Introducing the Future Now: Using Memetics and Popular Culture to Identify the Post-9/11 Homeland Security Zeitgeist.*

Choi, J. P., Jeon, D. S., & Kim, B.-C. (2015). Net Neutrality, Business Models, and Internet Interconnection. *American Economic Journal: Microeconomics, 7*, 104-141.

Conill, R. F. (2015). *Incorporating native advertising: Assessing journalism's new trend of camouflaging church as state.*

Friston, K. J., Lin, M., Frith, C., Pezzulo, G., Hobson, J. A., & Ondobaka, S. (2017). Active Inference, Curiosity and Insight. *Neural Computation, 29*, 2633-2683.

Gilder, G. (2019). *LIfe After Google. The Fall of Big Data and the rise -of the Blockhain Economy.* New York: Knopf.

Hanson, A. M. (1986). Ragtime: Its History, Composers, and Music by John Edward Hasse. *Indiana Magazine of History.*

Kaul, V. (2012). Changing Paradigms of Media Landscape in the Digital Age. *Journal of Mass Communication and Journalism.*

Loredana, P.-B. (2017). Inbound Marketing - the most important digital marketing strategy. *Bulletin of the Transilvania University of Brasov. Series V : Economic Sciences* (2), 61-68.

Munnukka, J., Uusitalo, O., & Jokela, E. (2014). *Advocacy participation and brand loyalty in virtual brand community.*

Pulipaka, L. K., Laigo, G. R., & Bhatti, A. H. (2016). *FLIPPED LEARNING: A PEDAGOGICAL APPROACH IN TEACHING MATHEMATICS.*

Pulipaka, R. (2016). *Design synthesis and anticancer activity of rutheniumII polypyridyl and piano stool type rutheniumII arene complexes.*

Tandoc, E. C., & Maitra, J. (2018). News organizations' use of Native Videos on Facebook: Tweaking the journalistic field one algorithm change at a time. *New Media & Society,* 1679-1696.

Tikno, T. (2018). Exploring the Acceptance for Pixel Technology Implementation in Facebook Ads among Advertisers in Indonesia. *KnE Social Sciences,*

Ventura, L. (2018). *The Reception of Hegel in Egypt and the "Spirit of Time" (Zeitgeist).*

Wilder, K. M. (2015). *Brand advocacy: Conceptualization and measurement.*

Kublach Haller

Kublach Haller Books are published by KHP Corporation, 7500 West 77th Street, Suite 35, Minneapolis, Minnesota with offices in Denver, Colorado and Columbia, South Carolina.

Made in the USA
Coppell, TX
09 May 2020